Antisocial personality Disorder

Learn to cope with people that has total disregard for others

By

Stella R. Thompson

MAIN THING

The information in this book is based on the author's knowledge, experience and opinions. The methods described in this book are not intended to be a definitive set of instructions. You may discover other methods and materials to accomplish the same end result. Your results may differ.

There are no representations or warranties, express or implied, about the completeness, accuracy, or reliability of the information, products, services, or related materials contained in this book. The information is provided "as is," to be used at your own risk.

All trademarks appearing in this book are the property of their respective owners.

This book may not be re-sold or given away to other people. If you like to share this book with another person, please purchase an additional copy for each person you share it with.

Chapter 1

Antisocial Personality Disorder (ASPD)

Antisocial personality disorder (ASPD) is a condition described by an absence of compassion and respect for others. Individuals who have Antisocial personality disorder have practically zero respect for right or wrong. They alienate and frequently act heartlessly or in a brutal way. People with this problem might lie, participate in a forceful or brutal way of behaving, and take part in the crime.

Individuals with Antisocial personality disorder (ASPD) can be clever, enchanting, and enjoyable to be near - - yet they can likewise lie and take advantage of others. Individuals with

ASPD seem cutthroat and don't show regret for their activities. Somebody with the issue might act imprudently, damagingly, and unsafely without feeling remorseful when their activities hurt others.

Present-day indicative frameworks consider ASPD to incorporate two related yet not indistinguishable circumstances: A "insane person" is somebody whose destructive activities toward others will generally reflect computation, control, and slyness; they likewise tend not to feel feeling and copy (as opposed to encounter) compassion for other people. It is an extreme type of ASPD. They can be misleading magnetic and enchanting. Conversely, "sociopaths" are to some degree more ready to shape connections to others yet dismiss social guidelines; they will generally be more incautious, random, and effortlessly upset than individuals with psychopathy. ASPD influences 2% to 4% of the populace and is more normal in men.

Understanding people with Antisocial Personality Disorder (ASPD)

character (ASPD) is one of the group B behavioral conditions, which normally include profound, rash, or emotional contemplations and activities. This gathering of behavioral conditions is likewise huge on the grounds that it incorporates marginal behavioral conditions (BPD) and self-centered behavioral conditions, notwithstanding ASPD. These issues, and behavioral conditions as a general rule, are among the most criticized emotional well-being conditions.

Conversationally, many individuals utilize the terms mental case and sociopath conversely with standoffish character. A typical supposition will be that all individuals who have ASPD are unequipped for feeling and believing and will ultimately perpetrate brutal wrongdoings and damage others. It's actually many individuals living with ASPD regularly don't feel regret or responsibility. They may likewise need compassion, the battle to grasp the feelings of others or experience continuous legitimate issues, because of a propensity toward rash and frequently hazardous or unlawful activities.

In any case, sociopathy is definitely not an emotional wellness determination, and few out of every odd individual with ASPD will hurt others or take part in fierce demonstrations. Workable for individuals who have ASPD to keep away from activities that could hurt others, particularly when they have support from a caring specialist. In treatment, individuals can foster relational abilities alongside adapting strategies for impulsivity and hostility. These instruments can help individuals who need to further develop connections and stay away from unlawful or hazardous actions and ways of behaving that hurt others.

Workable for individuals have ASPD to stay away from activities that could hurt others, particularly when they have support from a merciful specialist.

Chapter 2

How Common Is ASPD?

The assessed pervasiveness of ASPD might differ relying upon the review and models utilized. As per the Diagnostic and Statistical Manual of Mental Disorders (DSM-5), between around 0.2 and 3.3% of the populace has ASPD in a given year time span. This condition is just analyzed in individuals beyond 18 years old.

Over 90% of individuals determined to have ASPD additionally live with another psychological wellness issue. Substance misuse is the most well-known co-happening condition. The research proposes ASPD happens substantially more habitually in men determined to have liquor use jumble. Higher predominance is additionally found in jail settings, as well as populace tests from ruined regions. Other normal co-happening issues are tension and melancholy.

However ASPD is undeniably more uncommon in ladies than it is in men, some exploration has recommended when ASPD creates in ladies, the condition might turn out to be more extreme. Ladies living with ASPD are much more bound to mishandle substances than men living with ASPD. Be that as it may, research likewise demonstrates that withdrawn conduct might continue longer in men. Men who have ASPD additionally have an expanded gamble of early demise.

Forceful and fierce conduct in youth, for example, that seen with direct turmoil, can be a marker for ASPD. Not all youngsters who have led to confusion will proceed to foster ASPD, however, a background marked by direct turmoil is one of the indicative standards for ASPD. These side effects should show up before the age of 15. Parental disregard, misuse, irregularity, and an absence of soundness from essential guardians can all build the gamble that a kid with lead turmoil will foster ASPD.

Asocial Vs Antisocial

It's normal to hear solitary used to allude to individuals who like to be all alone and try not to invest a great deal of energy with others. Be that as it may, "asocial" is a more precise method for characterizing this indifference toward social cooperation. Asocial can portray an overall lack of engagement in the public eye and commitment to others, yet it doesn't show an individual harbors any hostility or negative expectation toward others.

Standoffish, then again, go past a general aversion or evasion of society and the local area. Individuals who meet standards for a determination of ASPD commonly feel unfriendly toward others. Indeed, even the individuals who don't have effectively threatening inclinations toward others might really focus almost no on the security, general prosperity, and sensations of most others. It's likewise normal for individuals who have standoffish attributes to have huge dismissal for their own security.

It's vital to take note that these sentiments don't be guaranteed to mean savage propensities. Investigations of individuals in jail really do uncover high paces of ASPD, yet this condition happens on a range, and not every person living with the condition becomes vicious or perilous. Research has additionally seen that certain individuals who show withdrawn characteristics might have fostered these ways of behaving to make due and safeguard themselves while experiencing childhood in troublesome conditions.

Many individuals use psychopathy as an equivalent for ASPD, yet this use isn't precise. Psychopathy can best be viewed as an extreme type of ASPD, instead of the most trademark show of the condition. The vast majority who meet measures for psychopathy as per the Psychopathy Checklist - Revised (PCL - R) do likewise meet standards for ASPD. However, just around 10% of individuals determined to have ASPD likewise meet rules for psychopathy.

At the center of ASPD lies a steady absence of respect for the privileges of others, which for the most part incorporates an imprudent, unreliable, and crazy way of behaving. Individuals might make a move disregarding possible outcomes and experience practically zero regrets for hurt brought about by their way of behaving. Robbery, control, and other trickery are normal, and individuals living with ASPD likewise will more often than not excuse or limit their activities.

Introverted conduct can incorporate fierce or criminal demonstrations, however, individuals living with ASPD aren't forceful or brutal 100% of the time. Also, while many individuals with ASPD need compassion, this isn't generally the situation. Individuals living with ASPD frequently battle to create or keep up with significant connections, and they might hurt their accomplices; however, it's as yet feasible for individuals with ASPD to feel love and compassion, frequently for a limited handful of individuals like youngsters, accomplices, or close relatives.

Misuse, disregard, or missing guardians can increment the risk for ASPD when different variables are available, especially beginning stage lead jumble. In individuals who foster ASPD, youth abuse can build up the conviction that no other person will pay special attention to them, so they ought to give their very best to take care of themselves and get their necessities met. This conviction normally happens with ASPD.

Lately, a couple of individuals with ASPD have expounded on their experience living with the condition. This might significantly affect the shame encompassing the condition, however many individuals actually battle to acknowledge that ASPD doesn't generally mean an individual is brutal or "evil." The disgrace related to behavioral conditions, ASPD specifically, may make it considerably more challenging for individuals who need to improve to get the assistance they with requiring. Negative perspectives from guardians and teachers might start almost immediately, frequently when youngsters first present indications of the lead issue.

The shame related to behavioral conditions, ASPD specifically, may make it significantly more challenging for individuals who need to improve to get the assistance they need. One with considering of 202 kindergarten educators found instructors were probably going to have an unforgiving reaction toward forceful kids. Be that as it may, negative perspectives, or discounting youngsters as miscreants or reprobates, can build up thoughts, for example, "I'm awful," "I won't ever add up to anything," or "Nobody tends to think about what befalls me," from youth. A few specialists accept this can expand the possibilities forceful way of behaving and negligence for others will proceed and decline.

Chapter 3

Diagnosis of Antisocial Personality Disorder

Antisocial personality disorder is analyzed in light of meeting rules portrayed in the Diagnostic and Statistical Manual on Mental Disorders, the book that psychological wellness experts use to survey patients. Albeit the fifth release (DSM-5) was distributed in 2012, a few clinicians keep on utilizing the fourth version (DSM-4) in making analyses.

In evaluating an individual for the Antisocial personality disorder, a psychological wellness expert will do a full mental assessment. This implies that the psychological wellness expert will pose the individual a progression of inquiries about their side effects and conduct. They will ask how serious the ways of behaving and side effects are, the way habitually they happen, and how long they have existed. They may likewise give the individual surveys to finish up, to see whether the individual meets the rules for other mental, conduct, character, or formative problems, noticed the National Institutes of Health.

No actual test, for example, a blood test or imaging, can be utilized to analyze Antisocial personality disorder. A few specialists have utilized cerebrum outputs to find ways that the minds of individuals with a determination of Antisocial personality disorder contrast from those of individuals with practically no psychological or behavioral conditions, however, it is basically impossible to utilize a sweep of an individual's cerebrum to decide if they have the condition.

A conclusion of Antisocial personality disorder might be remembered for a purported "differential finding," in that it likewise requires a clinician to preclude different circumstances which might show covering side effects, including bipolar confusion, consideration shortfall hyperactivity jumble (ADHD), and schizophrenia-related messes. In the same way as other circumstances, Antisocial personality disorder happens along a range. It isn't "available" or "missing," however an individual can have pretty much serious side effects.

Is There an ASPD Test?

You might see online ASPD tests, which incorporate a progression of inquiries regarding your character. These depend on DSM models that psychological wellness experts use to assist with diagnosing ASPD. These tests, nonetheless, commonly accompany the admonition that they're for "instructive" purposes as it were. They're not intended to replace an expert finding.

Finding Based on DSM-4 Criteria

To get a finding of Antisocial personality disorder as indicated by the DSM-4, an individual should meet four standards:

- Appearing "an unavoidable example of dismissal for and infringement of the freedoms of others happening since age 15 years"

- Age 18 or more seasoned
- Showing proof of direct problem before age 15
- Showing introverted conduct that isn't straightforwardly connected with schizophrenia or bipolar problem
- The example of dismissing others' freedoms is met by satisfying somewhere around three of the accompanying seven ways of behaving:
- Inability to adjust to accepted practices regarding legitimate ways of behaving, as demonstrated by more than once performing acts that are just for capture
- Underhandedness, as shown by continued lying, utilization of pseudonyms, or conning others for individual benefit or delight

- Impulsivity or inability to prepare Crabbiness and forcefulness, as demonstrated by rehashed actual battles or attacks
- Foolish dismissal for the wellbeing of self or others
- Predictable untrustworthiness, as demonstrated by the rehashed inability to support reliable work conduct or honor monetary commitments
- Absence of regret, as shown by being apathetic or think

The second and third rules, in regards to progress in years, remain closely connected: An individual who shows qualities of Antisocial personality disorder before age 18 ought to be determined to have direct confusion. A kid or juvenile with lead jumble has close-to-home and conduct issues, including resistance and imprudent way of behaving and an eagerness to disrupt guidelines and regulations, as per the National Institutes of wellbeing.

A clinician might determine an individual to have Antisocial personality disorder regardless of whether they get an authoritative determination of the lead problem, as long as their way of behaving before age 15 met the rules for direct turmoil.

Psychological well-being experts should likewise be certain that the lead problem isn't a misdiagnosis of another emotional wellness or formative condition. A kid with ADHD, for instance, might be misdiagnosed as having conduct jumble. The very side effects that lead to a direct problem conclusion may likewise be early side effects of the bipolar issue, schizophrenia, or significant burdensome issue.

Determination Based on DSM-5 Criteria

The models for the Antisocial personality disorder in the DSM-5, the latest version, are more mind-boggling and nuanced. It likewise eliminates the necessity for proof of lead problem before age 15. The DSM-5 characterizes an individual with Antisocial personality disorder as somebody something like 18 years of age who meets five different models:

1. Unfortunate Individual and Interpersonal Functioning

The individual priority issues with how they capability as an individual and with how they interface with others.

To show unfortunate working as an individual, they might be egocentric and base their confidence on private addition, power, or joy. Or then again they put forth objectives in view of how great it will cause them to feel without regard to its effect on others. They don't have an inward inspiration to keep social guidelines, regulations, or social morals.

An individual meets the measures for poor relational working by showing an absence of compassion or absence of closeness with others. They exhibit an absence of compassion by showing no worry for others' sentiments, needs, or enduring, and they need regret subsequent to harming another person.

Or then again their closeness shortage makes them unequipped for creating personal connections with others. All things being equal, they control, exploit, or control others for individuals increase by lying, threatening others, and constraining others to do what they need.

2. Hostility and Disinhibition

To meet the subsequent models, an individual high priority on two explicit character qualities: enmity and disinhibition.

They exhibit enmity by being manipulative, underhanded, insensitive, and threatening toward others. Their manipulativeness might include utilizing their appeal or mind to tempt or control others to meet some objective for themselves.

Underhandedness appears in regular deceiving others or embellishment about themselves. They might make things up while recounting a probably evident story, for instance.

Insensitivity alludes to showing no worry about others' sentiments or issues and not feeling responsibility or regret in the event that their activities hurt another person. They might be forceful or even cruel, enjoying others' aggravation.

Antagonism alludes to being every now and again furious or bad-tempered and looking for retribution for even minor abuses or unplanned mischief from others.

An individual with Antisocial personality disorder shows disinhibition through unreliability, impulsivity, and chance taking. They might break guarantees or neglect to meet monetary, business, individual, or social commitments, and they don't feel regret for these activities. They act immediately without thinking or thinking often about the potential outcomes of their activities or without an arrangement to manage those results.

They take part in risky exercises that might hurt themselves or others however without worrying about the potential outcomes. They might do such out of fatigue, to demonstrate that they can do something particularly unsafe, or on the grounds that they are trying to claim ignorance about their restrictions.

Notwithstanding the two measures over, an individual should meet every one of the three of the accompanying standards to get a finding of Antisocial personality disorder:

3. Predictable Behavior Across Time and Situations

Their concerns with individual and relational working portrayed above have happened all through their life in all circumstances. Their concerns don't disappear for specific periods or in specific circumstances.

4. No Other Psychological, Social, or Cultural Explanation

Their character issues and troubles in relational connections are not in any case made sense of by their phase of mental advancement or by their social or social climate. Assuming it would be typical for them to show these issues or attributes in light of their psychological turn of events or the social or social circumstances they live in, they wouldn't meet this prerequisite.

5. Conduct Not Caused by Substance Abuse or Medical Disorder

Their concerns are not a consequence of actual impacts from medications, liquor, or another substance, and they are not an aftereffect of another ailment, like a head injury or another psychological problem.

The most effective method to Treat Antisocial Personality Disorder
Antisocial personality disorder (ASPD) is a psychological well-being problem portrayed by a drawn-out example of controlling, taking advantage of, or abusing the freedoms of others with practically no regret. ASPD creates huge issues in connections and different everyday issues. Individuals with ASPD may likewise carry out criminal demonstrations.

ASPD is extremely difficult to treat. Frequently individuals with ASPD don't look for treatment except if they are expected to by a court. At the point when in treatment, they might be troublesome, unengaged, or even unfriendly toward the specialist.

No treatment has been demonstrated to be the best treatment for ASPD. There likewise is definitely not a first-line suggested treatment.

A few medicines have shown commitment, and certain individuals with ASPD see improvement in any event a portion of their side effects with treatment. Medicines that focus on specific ways of behaving and a few types of psychotherapy (talk treatment) mediations might help. Treating comorbid (coinciding) conditions, for example, temperament problems or substance use issues can likewise be gainful.

Chapter 4

Treatments for Antisocial Personality Disorder

There is a restricted exploration to help particular psychotherapy for the Antisocial personality disorder (ASPD), in spite of the fact that psychotherapy approaches are normally tried.

The objectives of treatment for ASPD are generally to help the individual:

- Deal with their negative ways of behaving
- Construct relational abilities and comprehend what their conduct means for other people

- Lessen rash ways of behaving that can prompt damage (to themselves or others) or capture

Treatment can include individual treatment for the individual, bunch treatment, family treatment, or a blend. Relatives and those near the individual with ASPD might track down esteem in treatment for themselves, as ASPD influences individuals near the individual with the condition as well.

Treatment may likewise include parts of outrage the board, substance use jumble treatment, and different medicines that target explicit side effects, ways of behaving, or comorbid conditions.

Mental Behavioral Therapy (CBT)

Mental conduct treatment (CBT) is a sort of psychotherapy. It includes assisting an individual with figuring out how to distinguish thinking examples and conduct that are maladaptive (not sufficient or suitable to the circumstance), broken (unusual), or generally undesirable. Over the long haul, under the direction of the advisor, the individual figures out how to change these risky reasoning examples and ways of behaving into ones that are better and more productive.

For individuals with ASPD, CBT might assist them with pondering what their conduct means to other people and what causes them problems.
CBT is presented as individual treatment, bunch treatment, as well as family treatment.

Mentalization-Based Treatment (MBT)
Individuals with ASPD frequently experience issues mentalizing (perceiving

and figuring out the psychological condition of themselves and others).
Mentalization-put together treatment centers with respect to the connection between the individual and the specialist. In this treatment, the advisor will zero in on the present as opposed to the past and will work with you to upgrade your close-to-home acknowledgment and association.

A recent report inspected the impacts of MBT on ASPD-related ways of behaving in patients with comorbid marginal behavioral conditions (BPD) and ASPD. The treatment included a year and a half of week-by-week consolidated individual and gathering psychotherapy meetings given by two different therapists.

The review found the members who got MBT encountered a decrease in frustration, antagonism, suspicion, and recurrence of self-damage and self-destruction endeavors, as well as an improvement in a pessimistic state of mind, general mental side effects, relational issues, and social change.

More exploration is required on what MBT means for individuals with ASPD, however, the outcomes are promising.

The creators of the review note that past exploration proposes the capacity to recognize others' feelings and goals might assist with social working and diminish the gamble of the standoffish way of behaving.

They additionally express that mentalizing has been displayed to safeguard against hostility in individuals with fierce characteristics and that reassuring mentalizing has been displayed to decrease school brutality.

Popularity-based Therapeutic Community (DTC)

As per some examinations, local area-based projects can be a successful long-haul treatment strategy for individuals with ASPD. It is turning out to be progressively utilized in jail settings, especially in Great Britain.

Popularity-based restorative local area (DTC) is a kind of friendly treatment including enormous and little treatment gatherings. It tends to the individual's close-to-home and mental requirements, as well as their gamble of perpetrating a criminal offense.

DTC centers around local area issues. In a jail setting, it expects to encourage a climate wherein both staff and imprisoned individuals add to the choices of the local area.

Rash Lifestyle Counseling

Rash way of life directing is a brief psychoeducational (the method involved with giving training and data to those chasing or getting psychological well-being administrations) program. It was produced for individuals with existing together ASPD and substance use jumble.

The program includes six one-hour meetings. It has been tried as an extra to short-term substance use jumble treatment, with promising outcomes.

The research proposes imprudent ways of life directing can further develop the probability the individual will remain in treatment and diminish substance utilization contrasted and commonplace treatment alone.

A 2015 preliminary found moderate momentary upgrades in substance use with the rash way of life guiding, proposing furnishing psychoeducation to short-term patients with Antisocial personality disorder would be helpful.

A recent report showed support for the utilization of hasty way of life guiding projects as a strategy for forestalling treatment dropout for patients with comorbid Antisocial personality disorder in substance use jumble treatment.

Doctor prescribed Medications for ASPD

There is no medicine supported for explicitly treating ASPD. Normally, in the event that a drug is endorsed, it is to focus on specific side effects, like hostility, despondency, or flighty temperaments, or to treat comorbid conditions.

A few prescriptions that might be endorsed to individuals with ASPD include:

- **Antidepressants**: These prescriptions can assist with controlling levels of specific temperament helping synapses in the cerebrum.
- **Antipsychotics**: This class of medications might assist with controlling hasty hostility.

- **Mind-set stabilizers:** These medications assist with overseeing extreme changes in temperament.

A 2020 survey of concentrates on utilizing medicine to treat ASPD observed that the dependability of current information is exceptionally low and that there was insufficient proof to decide if the drug is compelling for treating individuals with ASPD.

More examination is expected to figure out which prescriptions if any, are suggested for the treatment of ASPD. Meanwhile, individuals with ASPD ought to talk about the entirety of their side effects with their medical care supplier or psychological wellness expert to check whether the prescription might work out great for themselves as well as their requirements.

ASPD is hard to treat and there are no plainly approved treatments or meds demonstrated explicitly for treating it.

Certain individuals with ASPD track down treatment or potentially medicine helps them, particularly for specific side effects and for comorbid conditions.

For certain individuals with ASPD, certain side effects develop their own when they arrive in their 40s.

Chapter 5

Coping With an Antisocial Personality Disorder patient

We have all heard a cheerful joke made to the detriment of an especially bashful, peaceful, and hermitic individual. Somebody will teasingly say, "She has Antisocial personality disorder." It is a typical confusion that standoffish problem is just a repugnance for social circumstances or maybe an outrageous cumbersomeness in group environments, nonetheless, Antisocial personality disorder is very troublesome. As per the American Psychiatric Association (APA), the people who are analyzed as having a solitary character will generally be, "manipulative, unpredictable, troublesome and frequently draw in is forceful, rash 'carrying on' ways of behaving, which might remember attacks for other people, self-mutilation and some of the time self-destruction endeavors." An example of a problematic way of behaving can be obvious in an individual as youthful as the age of 15, in any case, an individual can't be clinically determined to have Antisocial personality disorder until they are 18 years of age. Assuming you suspect that a friend or family member is battling this problem, there are a couple of things you can do to help the person in question adapt.

1. Perceive the Symptoms

The individuals who have an introverted character are portrayed as having an outrageous dismissal of individuals' freedoms and are known to disregard the privileges of others consistently. This conduct is outlined with a large number of intense side effects, including an absence of regret, crabbiness, forcefulness, inability to adjust to normal practices, underhandedness, wild negligence, impulsivity, and consistent recklessness.

An absence of regret can be described by the people who show a lack of concern in the wake of having harmed somebody truly, intellectually, or inwardly.

Crabbiness and forcefulness are frequently shown by rehashed physical/verbal battles or attacks. A portion of the side effects of the reserved issue might seem like character peculiarities or run-of-the-mill credits of young disobedience, for instance, the inability to adjust to normal practices. As an eyewitness, you should be sufficiently clever to differentiate between a youthful grown-up carrying on as youngsters frequently do and a youthful grown-up over and over-performing acts that are just for capture - which shows powerlessness to adjust to normal practices. Underhandedness might be one of the more terrible parts of Antisocial personality disorder for the loved ones of the analyzed; this characteristic is delineated by over and again lying or controlling friends and family for individual increase or joy.

A considerable lot of the side effects can become perilous not just for the individual beset with the behavioral condition, yet additionally for those near the person. At the point when a singular starts showing crazy dismissal for their own wellbeing and for the security of people around them, it can turn out to be extremely troubling and risky, particularly when combined with impulsivity. Another side effect, steady recklessness, may seem like another of those characteristics that can undoubtedly be excused as a quality common by many individuals, particularly school mature people, yet loved ones might start to feel the heaviness of the side effects themselves. At the point when friends and family need to continually get a move on for their companion or relative by respecting their monetary commitments or rationalizing to their managers for them concerning why they neglect to support steady work conduct, now is the ideal time to pay heed and make a move.

2. Make a move

It might shock no one that the people who have the qualities of an introverted character don't look for treatment all alone. On the off chance that you are worried about a friend or family member and you feel they have every one of the side effects of Antisocial personality disorder, it is exhorted that you ask them to look for treatment. A few experts even propose giving the individual a rundown of outcomes that you will stick to on the off chance that they don't look for treatment, similar to those giving a mediation for a dependent individual to medications or liquor are encouraged to do. Intercession is a shrewd move to make during the underlying phases of endeavoring to help your cherished one. They frequently don't work, however, in the uncommon situation that mediation takes care of business, it can end up being extremely advantageous. In the event that an individual doesn't eagerly go into the treatment with Antisocial personality disorder, the following stage is having treatment court commanded, which can be a long and laborious cycle that makes the family lose valuable time that could somehow be utilized to help their cherished one out of luck.

A large number of those in treatment for the Antisocial personality disorder are court references. At the point when a court alludes to an individual idea to have the problem, they are shipped off to an office to be surveyed through a progression of tests and tests. In the event that the individual is determined to have Antisocial personality disorder, they are commanded to treatment.

Antisocial personality disorder is described by disturbing and misread side effects. For instance, an unavoidable absence of regret is normal in people who experience the ill effects of Antisocial personality disorder and it frequently shows up as though the individual has no sentiments by any means, which isn't true. These kinds of side effects make the issue undeniably challenging to treat and those with the ailment are frequently exposed to abuse and misdiagnosis. Antisocial personality disorder is likewise regularly mistaken for comparative problems, like sociopathic and psychopathic issues.

The most effective way to make heads or tails of a withdrawn character is psychotherapy. One would expect that drug is the principal suggestion, yet shockingly, "there is no exploration that upholds the utilization of prescriptions for direct treatment of Antisocial personality disorder," psychcentral.com reports. The most helpful sort of treatment for an individual determined to have Antisocial personality disorder will happen in a short-term setting where meetings can be committed to sharing and examining the qualities of their issue. Individuals who experience the ill effects of Antisocial personality disorder miss the mark on the capacity to figure out the results of their activities. They find it hard to see the relationship between sentiments and conduct.

3. Figure out how to Accept

At the point when a relative or other cherished one chooses, or at times, is compelled to go into treatment with Antisocial personality disorder, it is essential to be steady and stay hopeful. Current discoveries recommend that

Antisocial personality disorder is hereditary, hence ready to be dealt with and managed, yet never "restored." The determined individual generally battles to understand the connection among ways of behaving and sentiments and how their activities can cause torment, either substantial or close to home, to everyone around them and to themselves.

While clearly, you can't switch off your affections for the individual who has been analyzed as standoffish, your limits with this individual must stay clear. Likewise, you should understand that the individual's ailment might deteriorate before it improves. It isn't the least bit unprecedented for patients to be treated with Antisocial personality disorder rejecting treatment at first. However there is no particular drug that fixes the problem, meds are frequently recommended to help with specific side effects of the issue. For instance, antidepressants and temperament stabilizers might be useful in treating wretchedness or other psychological wellness gives that are normal in the people who experience the ill effects of Antisocial personality disorder.

The affection and backing of loved ones are the best medication for those experiencing Antisocial personality disorder. If at any time you feel alone, overpowered, or have sensations of responsibility about your companion or relative experiencing the issue, there are many care groups that can be tracked down on the web or locally.

The most effective method to assist somebody with an Antisocial behavioral condition

Antisocial personality disorder is portrayed in a rash, wild, and disastrous way of behaving. Individuals with this frequently have no sympathy or an absence of sentiments, and they control or hurt individuals. They frequently participate in the criminal way of behaving, which prompts issues with the law or prison time. Antisocial personality disorder is viewed as one of the most troublesome behavioral conditions to treat. To assist your adored one, you with canning attempt to urge them to seek treatment, support them as they go through treatment, and put down stopping points to deal with yourself.

Chapter 6

Helping an Antisocial personality disorder patient

Empowering Treatment

Find out about Antisocial personality disorder. One method for aiding your cherished one and urge treatment is to find out as much about the confusion as possible. Individuals with Antisocial personality disorder frequently appear to ignore or abuse others, neglect to comply with rules and accepted practices and have no regret.

Those with Antisocial personality disorder are frequently underhanded and manipulative. They falsehood, take, or con individuals for their benefit.

They frequently are imprudent, wild, and forceful, which prompts battles.

Converse with a specialist or advisor about the Antisocial personality disorder, or search on the web or purchase books to learn about the turmoil.

Antisocial personality disorder is portrayed as a rash, foolish, and disastrous way of behaving. Individuals with this frequently have no sympathy or an absence of sentiments, and they control or hurt individuals. They frequently participate in the criminal way of behaving, which prompts issues with the law or prison time. Antisocial personality disorder is viewed as one of the most troublesome behavioral conditions to treat. To assist your adored one, you with canning attempt to urge them to seek treatment, support them as they go through treatment, and put down stopping points to deal with yourself

1. Find out about Antisocial personality disorder. One method for aiding your adored one and urge treatment is to find out as much about the turmoil as possible. Individuals with Antisocial personality disorder frequently appear to dismiss or abuse others, neglect to comply with rules and accepted practices and have no regret.
Those with Antisocial personality disorder are frequently underhanded and manipulative. They untruth, take, or con individuals for their benefit.
They frequently are indiscreet, foolish, and forceful, which prompts battles.
Converse with a specialist or specialist about the Antisocial personality disorder, or search on the web or purchase books to learn about the confusion.

2. Propose treatment. Because of the idea of Antisocial personality disorder, many individuals with the condition won't look for treatment. You can attempt to propose that your adored one find support for their behavioral condition. Make sense that you care about them and believe they should find support for their way of behaving.

Many individuals with this problem will possibly look for treatment whenever compelled to by a court framework.

Since one of the side effects of ASPD is doubt and abhorrence of power figures, frequently the individual sees a specialist or specialist as a power figure they can't confide in. This prompts a terrible relationship.

Take a stab at saying, "I care about you, and your way of behaving has begun to concern me. I figure you would profit from clinical treatment."

3. Support psychotherapy. Psychotherapy is the most widely recognized treatment for the Antisocial personality disorder. In treatment, the advisor will work with the individual to put forth objectives, further develop connections, and foster adapting abilities. Treatment will likewise address your adored one's sentiments or absence of sentiments, alongside their standoffish inclinations.

Treatment may likewise chip away at attempting to interface conduct with sentiments or feelings.

4. Propose a care group. Support gatherings can be extremely useful in the event that your cherished one finds the right care group. The care group ought to be centered explicitly around reserved conduct jumble. This will allow your cherished one an opportunity to interface with others going through comparable circumstances and offer their encounters.

In a care group not custom-made explicitly to ASPD, your cherished one might stay segregated and sincerely far off. Some care groups can transform into where they build up a bad way of behaving, such as discussing how to participate in the criminal way of behaving.

Converse with your cherished one's primary care physician or a nearby medical clinic to attempt to track down a gathering in your space. You can likewise look online for a care group in your space.

5. Try not to take steps to get your adored one to go to treatment. Your adored one probably shouldn't go to treatment, even after you have attempted to persuade them to. If so, don't attempt to compromise the individual to make them look for treatment. This will just drive an individual with ASPD further away and make them safer.

You might feel enticed to give your cherished one danger like you will tell the court they are not consistence with their orders in the event that they don't go to treatment.

Rather than undermining, attempt to help your cherished one concoct motivations to proceed or begin treatment. You might make sense of that on the off chance that they go to treatment that they have a superior possibility of escaping issues with the general set of laws and not going to prison once more.

6. Be ready for any response. Individuals with behavioral conditions frequently experience difficulty tolerating that they have a problem. Somebody with Antisocial personality disorder might disapprove of this thought because of the idea of the issue. At the point when you approach an individual with ASPD about treatment, be ready for any reaction.

Certain individuals may not realize they have an issue, so you might need to give instances of their ways of behaving. Others might be trying to claim ignorance or decline to accept there is an issue.

Certain individuals with ASPD might be safe or furious assuming that you raise the likelihood that they have a behavioral condition.

Offering Help

1. Support your cherished one through treatment. Assuming your adored one consents to treatment, it may not be simple for them. Many individuals with ASPD have no compassion or an absence of sentiments. This can make it challenging for them when they begin reaching out to their sentiments or attempting to explore feelings. Offer love and backing for your adored ones as they go through this cycle. Treatment might be trying for your adored one on occasion. They might get overpowered or upset, or they might get baffled and need to stop. Keep empowering them and being there however much you can.

2. Be comprehension of your adored one through close-to-home revelation. As your cherished one attempts to reveal feelings and become happier with feeling them, they might go through a ton of close-to-home cycles. Be strong of this multitude of feelings on the grounds that any feeling that isn't outrage or bothering is something to be thankful for.

For instance, many individuals with ASPD wind up feeling discouraged for a brief time. Assist them with understanding and distinguishing that these feelings are associated with wretchedness or pity.

Be steady with them during this time by getting it, tuning in, and assisting them in any capacity they with expecting to.

3.   Construct a close-to-home association. One thing that might be finished to help your adored one is to deal with building a close-to-home association. A great many people with ASPD do have not many genuinely critical connections in their lives. You might attempt to construct a profound association with your adored one.

You might have to work with a specialist to track down ways of interfacing sincerely with your cherished one.

You can't cause your adored one to feel feelings or begin to address their feelings. This must be finished with the assistance of a specialist. When your adored one begins to embrace their feelings, you can begin to attempt to interface with them.

4. Make them face their outcomes. One way you can assist your adored one with figuring out how to adapt and acknowledge their condition is to assist them with confronting the results of their activities. For an individual with Antisocial personality disorder, this is in many cases outrageous, similar to imprisonment or through the general set of laws.

Make your adored one mindful of the horrendous conduct they are taking part in, such as lying or taking, getting into battles, or harming their friends and family.

Dealing with Yourself

1. Look for treatment for yourself. Since those with ASPD can genuinely, intellectually, or sincerely hurt you, you ought to look for psychological wellness treatment for yourself. Chatting with a specialist can assist you with managing your perplexing feelings and master adapting abilities.
You might have to figure out how to define limits or safeguard yourself.

2. Go to family treatment. Family treatment can be extremely useful when your cherished one has Antisocial personality disorder. Family treatment can assist you and other relatives with looking into your cherished one's problem and figuring out how to help. Family treatment may likewise assist you with seeing more about your cherished one's mentality and character.

ASPD can cause a lot of misconceptions and disarray for friends and family. Family treatment might give you a spot to communicate your sentiments, figure out how to collaborate with your cherished one, and adapt to your sentiments.

You may likewise attempt a care group for groups of those with Antisocial personality disorder.

3. Put down stopping points. You might need to define limits with your adored one because of their way of behaving. These limits are made to safeguard your physical, mental, and close-to-home prosperity. Be clear in what your limits are and demand that your cherished ones regard your limits.

Your adored one might be forcefully vicious, which might prompt actual damage to you or other relatives. They may likewise be pointlessly wild and placed individuals in hurt. You might need to concoct actual limits, such as just seeing them at specific times. You might need to request that they not shout at you, genuinely contact you, or hit you. You may likewise need to decline to ride in a vehicle with them, for instance. Take a stab at saying, "I'm willing to talk, yet you won't contact me or shout at me."

Your adored one might control you, falsehood, or take. They might do or express things to hurt you or harm your relationship. This might prompt close-to-home or mental limits. You might need to separate yourself or tell your adored one, "We can see one another, however not in the event that you will holler at me or lie to me."

Individuals with ASPD might exploit any mindfulness or empathy. You might have to safeguard yourself by defining limits for yourself. You might say, "I care about you and back your treatment, yet I won't permit you to exploit me."

4. Track down an emotionally supportive network. You will likely feel many feelings as you attempt to persuade your adored one to look for treatment and attempt to think about their behavioral condition. You might feel sad, miserable, or discouraged. You ought to find an emotionally supportive network of individuals you can rest on and converse with when you get overpowered.

These individuals might be companions or family who are associated with your adored one, or individuals who don't know them by any stretch of the imagination. You might request other relatives or companions from your cherished one to help you. You can't do everything without help from anyone else.

5. Make a stride back. There might come when you really want to make a stride back. Your cherished one might be impervious to treatment, trying to claim ignorance that something is off-base, or taking part in a damaging or unsafe way of behaving. Your cherished one might be lying and taking from you, mistreating you, or controlling you. In the event that you end up in a distressing circumstance, risky circumstance, or circumstance where you feel dangerous, make a stride back.

This implies you might need to eliminate yourself from your adored one's life or do another thing to guarantee your security and profound prosperity.